Spotlight On The Minor Prophets: Bible Study – 12 Book Bundle

Twelve Books in one: Jonah, Obadiah, Joel, Hosea, Amos, Micah, Nahum, Zephaniah, Habakkuk, Haggai, Zechariah, Malachi

BY
James Paris

Illustrations By

Agnieszka Gorak

Updated August 2016

ISBN-10: 1492317780
ISBN-13: 978-1492317784

Table of Contents

Contents

COPYRIGHT

Published By
Deanburn Publications

www.TheBibleBrief.com

Introduction

"Give instruction to a wise man, and he will be still wiser; teach a righteous man, and he will increase in learning." Proverbs 9:9

It must be registered from the outset that this is an outline Bible study only, of the so called 'Minor Prophets'; written as an introduction to a small group of people who played a huge role in guiding/warning the nations of Israel and Judah of The Lords will regarding them.

It is not intended to be an in-depth expose but rather a 'taster' in the ministry of the Lord through the written works of his servants the prophets. It is written in such a way that discussion is encouraged, and questions asked as well as answered.

As such I am sure that the readers themselves, with just a little study would be able to expand considerably the material presented here – which is in fact the intention of this modest work.

Each Prophet will be considered individually, the intention being to create an overall work in the form of twelve individual books, covering the twelve prophets.

Are they relevant for Christian study today ? Well quite apart from such scriptures as "all scripture is God breathed...." 2 Tim 3:16 here are just a few examples that stand out...

- Habakkuk 2:4 "The just shall live by his faith" Sparked the Reformation under Martin Luther.
- Zechariah 11:12 Gave us the price of a slave – 30 pieces of silver, and many other details relating to the coming messiah.
- Joel 2,3 warns us of the 'last days' and the trials to come.
- Malachi 3:1 reveals the ministry of John the Baptist and the fact that he would come again to herald the return of the Messiah.

The Prophets.

First of all it must be emphasised that the title of 'Minor Prophets' does not in any way place these individuals and the instructions that they gave, in an inferior category to the 'Majors' such as Isaiah or Jeremiah.

The 'minor' title really just applies to the brevity of the messages given by these Prophets in relation to their more wordy brothers, and is thought to originate in Augustine's time (4th C.)

Up until then the whole Old Testament was referred to as 'The law and the Prophets' which included also the 'Writings'.

In the Jewish canon what we call the 'Minor' Prophets are simply known as the 'twelve' and are listed amongst the other Prophets.

God is not impressed by our many words but rather our faithfulness to the calling into which he has called us – something to be borne in mind !

The Purpose:

The purpose of this work, as alluded to earlier, is not to write yet another commentary or theological discourse on the minor prophets. The purpose rather is to inspire debate and discussion, perhaps in a home bible study group, that will lead to a better understanding not only of the times and circumstances in which the prophets lived and ministered; but in fact a better understanding of where we are right now.

This work is in fact **intended to be incomplete**, and if doing the purpose for which it was conceived, should lead to many questions and discussions ! For this reason at the end, and throughout the books I have included some questions that should be brought to the group, to inspire and prayerfully consider the answers given by the rest of the group.

In many countries, apathy – not persecution - is the biggest enemy of the word of God in the times in which we find ourselves. Intelligent conversation, even heated argument is needed, if we are not to be sucked into an apathetic Christianity that is quite happy to see the unbelieving world slip away into a lost eternity.

Dates

In the following chart I have endeavoured to place a time around which the various prophets ministered. It should be understood that in a few of the cases i.e. Obadiah, there may be considerable debate as to the actual dating of the book, in these instances I have taken the 'path of least resistance' and chosen the most universally accepted date.

There may also be some debate as to when the books were actually written i.e. some suggest that they were written after the actual events. Thankfully it is not within the remit of this introductory work to investigate these possibilities! I have chosen therefore to select the most appropriate time in relation to the prophet involved with the book.

However do feel free to disagree; remember this work is all about intelligent debate leading to understanding – eventually !

As for the order of the prophets, as they appear in this work. I have begun with the prophet Jonah – why ? because he is my favourite !

Yes it's terrible to have favourites I know, but that's just the way I am. Jonah makes me laugh, and he makes me sad. The important thing is that he makes me something ! Remember apathy? I can relate to Jonah and his frustrations and fears. Maybe you can relate better to Joel, or Malachi perhaps ? I would count it as a great success if after this study, you are able to relate a little better with any of the very real characters found within this group, we know as the minor prophets.

After Jonah, we will revert to studying in a more orderly fashion, as this does help to get a better 'handle' on what and who was where at any given time in history.

Timeline

Here in the chart below is a timeline, that will help with understanding just who was king at the time of the prophet's ministry; as well as other relevant details.

Prophet	Date (B.C.)	Name Meaning	Prophesies to/about	King at Time (Assumption)
Obadiah	845-750	Servant of The Lord	Israel / Edom	Jehoram (Judah) Joram (Israel)
Joel	835-796	Yahweh is God	Judah	Joash (Judah) Jehu/Jehoahaz (Israel)
Jonah	793-753	Dove	Nineveh	Jotham/Ahaz (Judah) Jeroboam/Pekah/Hoshea (Israel)
Hosea	753-715	Salvation	Israel	Jotham/Uzziah (Judah)
Amos	760-755	Burden Bearer	Israel / Judah	Jeroboam/Pekah (Israel)
Micah	770-710	Who is like unto The Lord	Israel / Judah	Jotham/Ahaz/Hezekiah (Judah) Zechariah/Hoshea (Israel)
Nahum	655	Consolation	Nineveh	Manasseh (Judah)*
Zephaniah	625	Yahweh Hides	Judah, Assyria & Nations	Josiah (Judah)
Habakkuk	610	Clings To	Judah / Nations	Josiah/Jehoahaz/Jehoiakim
Haggai	520	My Feast	Judah	N/A
Zechariah	520	Yahweh has remembered	Judah	N/A
Malachi	460-420	My Messenger	Judah	N/A

- Manasseh deserves 'special' mention here as he is recorded as the most evil king that Judah ever had (2 Kings 21) - and yet he repented and turned to the LORD in the last years of his reign.

Book 1: JONAH

"Arise, go to Nineveh, that great city, and cry against it;

for their wickedness is come up before me." Jonah 1.2

BACKGROUND:

Based around 780 BC, the book of Jonah is written during the time of reign of Jeroboam 11. Jonah is mentioned in 11 Kings 14:25.

This was a time when the Assyrian empire was reaching its most powerful.

Nineveh eventually conquered and took into captivity the northern kingdom of Israel in 722-721 BC

Nineveh itself was a massive city and is recorded as being around 7 miles in circumference with stone walls and towers over 200 feet high and 50 feet thick – wide enough for 6-7 chariots abreast; enabling quick defense to any part of the wall that was threatened. The city is first mentioned in Genesis 10:11 as being founded by the hunter Nimrod, who also built the tower of Babel and so instituted a rebellion against God. From this we see that the city of Nimrod (Nineveh) is always seen in a negative light, when it comes to the worship of the true God.

Famous for the worship of Ishtar (Astarte) the fertility goddess, the city of Nineveh was also full of temples (around 2,000) to many different deities including Sin, Nerbal, Shamash, and Nabu – just to name a few. The Assyrians themselves had a well-deserved reputation for utter ruthlessness and barbarity, towards any who stood against them.

It was into this situation that The Lord decided to send Jonah, with a message to repent or be judged. In fact The Lord gave them 40 days until they faced utter destruction, but Jonah knew that if they repented then God would forgive, as he complains here.."

"Isn't this what I said, Lord, when I was still at home? That is what I tried to forestall by fleeing to Tarshish. I knew that you are a gracious and compassionate God, slow to anger and abounding in love, a God who relents from sending calamity. 3 Now, Lord, take away my life, for it is better for me to die than to live." Jonah 4:2

Jonah has been described as a complete bigot by some, and a patriot by others, both standpoints have their merits. However put yourself in Jonah's shoes before judging to harshly, or indeed commending too loudly.

The Ninevites were the sworn enemies of the Israelites, indeed they were the persecutors of many nations at that time. They worshiped false idols, offering human sacrifice and worship through temple prostitutes. In the eyes of a man of God such as Jonah, the Assyrians were an abomination worthy of the full measure of a righteous God's wrath.

Imagine for a moment if you as a Christian, had a neighbor who worshiped the devil, beat you up whenever you passed, and from whom you had to hide your daughters – then the Lord comes to you one night and says he is going to judge them for their wickedness…and you're to take the news! The problem is that you know they are likely to repent and be forgiven – what would you do ?

Before going further discuss this with the group for a few minutes, and gauge the reactions.

Jonah's Journey

*"Let my words, like vegetables, be tender and sweet, for tomorrow I may have to eat them." - **Author Unknown***

The story of Jonah is familiar to millions worldwide. It transcends racial, religious and cultural boundaries inasmuch as it is steeped into the collective consciences of millions world-wide. To be a Jonah, is to be someone who is cursing all those around them by their very presence. Sailors even to this day refer regularly to someone 'being a Jonah' if they have suffered a series of misfortunes.

What's in a name: Jonah means 'Dove' or messenger. Fundamentally that is what he was, a simple messenger of the Lord – and a very effective one at that.

Story in a nutshell

The Lord has seen the wickedness of the people of Nineveh, and decided to judge them for their wickedness. Jonah is chosen to be the messenger to the Ninevites. He is however not happy with his task and immediately runs from the presence of God.

In the process of running from his mission, Jonah jumps on board a trading ship heading for Tarshish, which unsurprisingly is in the opposite direction to Nineveh.

A storm brews up threatening to sink the ship which results in the crew drawing lots, to see who had brought this calamity upon them. Jonah is pointed out and confesses that it is his fault, telling them to throw him overboard to prevent any further disaster. The crew reluctantly agree, Jonah is thrown overboard straight into the mouth of a giant fish, that keeps him there for three days, when Jonah finally repents.

"In my distress I called to the Lord,
and he answered me.
From deep in the realm of the dead I called for help,
and you listened to my cry." **Jonah 2:1**

He is puked up on the shore near the city of Nineveh, and his remarkable ministry causes everyone to repent in sackcloth and ashes – including the King and even the animals of the field.

God hears the cry of the Ninevites and their repentant heart, and decides to forgive them their sins – Jonah is hopping mad. Hoping to change God's mind Jonah sits down under a vine shelter, that the Lord has caused to grow up, in order to await the destruction of Nineveh.

A worm comes, kills the vine, Jonah is roasted under the hot sun and says to The Lord *"It would be better for me to die than to live."* **Jonah 4:8**

The story end by God pointing out to Jonah that there is a lot more at stake than perhaps Jonah is thinking about.

"You have been concerned about this plant, though you did not tend it or make it grow. It sprang up overnight and died overnight. And should I not have concern for the great city of Nineveh, in which there are more than a hundred and twenty thousand people who cannot tell their right hand from their left—and also many animals?" **Jonah4:10**

MAIN POINTS:

- God sees the wickedness of Nineveh and determines to judge it.
- Calls on Jonah to warn of impending doom.
- Jonah does a runner – ends up in the belly of giant fish.
- Jonah repents and goes (reluctantly) to deliver the message.
- Ninevites believe Jonah's message and repent in sackcloth and ashes-even the King.
- Jonah not happy – just wants to sit down and die!

Points For Discussion – Group Input

"But love your enemies, do good to them, and lend to them without expecting to get anything back. Then your reward will be great, and you will be children of the

Most High, because he is kind to the ungrateful and wicked." **Luke 6:35**

Q1 – Why would The Lord care about the Ninevites, the great persecutors of Israel?

First Clue.........'For God so loved the WORLD ......' (John 3:16)

Discuss>>>>>>>Jews thought that The Lord loved only them…Whereas he is the God of all the world. Danger in judging people who may or may not be 'worthy' !!

Q2 – Why did The Lord choose Jonah, and why did he run?

Answer…..Why Not !! The lord is no respecter of persons (acts 10:34)

Often he will choose the weak to defeat the strong (witness the story of David vs. Goliath) or the foolish to confound the wise (1 cor 1:27) **Get someone to read**.

My own experience: I was once told that 'God would not use you if you do not love the people" Utter Nonsense !……..**discuss** - many ways to love people. Jonah being the prime example of someone who did not love the people but God used him anyway.

Why did Jonah run?

Firstly, Jonah had every good reason (he thought) to wish Gods judgment on the Ninevites.

They were the great tyrants of the Middle East, the persecutors of Israel, an ungodly mob fully deserving of HIS God's wrath.

Secondly, Jonah 4:2 **Get someone to read** 'slow to anger and abounding in loving kindness'(Jonah 4:2) . He (Jonah) was right !

Q3 – Why did they believe Jonah ?
Answer: The story of Jonah was probably known to the Ninevites.

His story had gone before him. Remember we are talking about a man who had been puked up alive on a beach, from the mouth of a giant fish. There was more than likely witnesses to this 'beaching'. Apart from which there is no doubt that the stories from the sailors themselves would have travelled far and wide.

When the Ninevites saw Jonah, they were more than ready to hear his message…Gods planning perhaps ?

SUMMARY - LESSONS

1 – " For God so loved the world" The Lord loves and wishes everyone to come to repentance. (1 john 1:9 if we confess our sins….).
Repentance = Deliverance.

2 – God can and does, call on all kinds of people to accomplish his will. This book tells the story of a reluctant prophet who arguably becomes one of the most effective preachers in the entire Bible – and he was not happy about it !

SPOTLIGHT ON THE MINOR PROPHETS

Book 2

Obadiah

Part 2 of a Christian home-group
discussion course on the 12 Prophets

James Paris

Book 2: OBADIAH

History/Background

The year is approx. 845 B.C. I must point out that there is doubt surrounding this date as there is dispute over whether Obadiah is referring to the sacking of Jerusalem by Nebuchadnezzar in 586 BC or in fact referring to 845 BC when Jerusalem was attacked by the Philistines and the Arabs. As such, this book is one of the most difficult to date with accuracy.

For this work though I have chosen the 845 BC date. Either way, it has no significant influence on the message given by the Prophet Obadiah.

The Situation:

Israel has been split into two kingdoms after the death in 925 B.C. of King Solomon.

King Solomon in his later years had ruled Israel with a rod of iron, partially enslaving his own people in order to complete his immense building projects and serve his ever-growing army of administrators and lackeys. This caused huge resentment amongst the common people who thought that the death of King Solomon – as sad as it was – would lead to an easing of the burden that they were under.

Unfortunately this was not to be the case as his heir Rehoboam, promised even harsher discipline when he took over the reins of power.

" My father made your yoke heavy, but I will add to your yoke; my father disciplined you with whips, but I will discipline you with scorpions."
1 Kings 12:14

As you may imagine, this did not go down at all well, and indeed was against the advice of his elders. This resulted in ten tribes going their own way, and forming the Northern kingdom of Israel with the late King Solomon's labour advisor Jeroboam as their King.

Question To Ask – What would you have done in the Israelites situation; stayed on to get beaten and abused, or risk moving to a better, if uncertain future?

The southern Kingdom is ruled by Solomon's son Rehoboam and is named Judah.

Eighty years later
We pick-up now at the time of Obadiah. Jerusalem at this time (845 B.C.) had just been attacked and looted by the Philistines and the Arabs supported by Edom.

The Book
What's in a name? Obadiah means 'Servant of the Lord' or 'One who serves'
Shortest book in the Old Testament.

Point of note – this is one of the 7 Old Testament books that are not quoted in the NT.
However it is quoted in several places by the prophet Joel and Jeremiah. Cf Joel 2:32, Jeremiah 49:14

Subject matter is of course God's judgment!
This time however it is not the usual suspects i.e. the Israelites or Assyria but instead it is against the Edomites.

Who were the Edomites?

They were the descendants of Esau - Jacobs's brother.
The pair being the late sons of Isaac and Rebekah.
Right from the get go there was conflict between the two brothers (Gen 25:22,23) READ
This conflict continued throughout their history:-
• Jacob talked Esau out of his birthright for a plate of stew. (Gen 25:27-34)
• He tricked his father Isaac into blessing him instead of Esau. (Gen 27)
• There was potential for real trouble when the brothers met years later. (Gen 32-33)
• Conflict at the time of the Exodus when Edom refused the Israelites safe passage through their land. (Num 20:14-21)

- Enmity continued with King David (11 Samuel 8:14)
- During the reign of Jehoram Edom revolts and sets up their own King (11 Kings 8:20-22) about 845 B.C. Obadiah gives this prophecy to the Edomites. Points of note:-
- 'Edom' means Red – the color of the stew for which he sold his birthright.
- Much of the land owned by the Edomites was made up of dark red sandstone. The ancient city of Petra, with its stone buildings carved out of solid stone, being the most famous example for us today.
- This was also the color of Esau at his birth (Gen 25:25).

Why does Obadiah preach God's judgment on them?

READ Obadiah 1:10-*11* *"Because of violence to your brother Jacob,*
You will be covered with shame,

And you will be cut off forever.
[11] "On the day that you stood aloof,
On the day that strangers carried off his wealth,
And foreigners entered his gate
And cast lots for Jerusalem—
You too were as one of them…"

The city of Jerusalem had been attacked by the Philistines and Arabians. The city had been stormed and looted. Edom, who was in a state of revolt, sided with the invading forces and shared in the spoils (Obad. 11). They gloated over Israel's misfortune (Obad. 12-13), and killed or imprisoned those who fled the destruction (Obad. 14).

V18 Read. Also Malachi 1:3-4 .. *"but I have hated Esau, and I have made his mountains a desolation and* *appointed his inheritance for the jackals of the wilderness." 4 Though Edom says, "We have been beaten down, but we will return and build up the ruins"; thus says the Lord of hosts, "They may build, but I will tear down; and men will call them the wicked territory, and the people toward whom the Lord is indignant forever."*

Question To Ask
When did the final confrontation between Jacob and Esau takes place?
Answer: During the trial of Jesus Christ, when Jesus (a descendant of Jacob) stood before King Herod (a descendant of Esau).
Who does God use to judge? v7 *"All the men allied with you Will send you forth to the border, and the men at peace with you Will deceive you and overpower you. They who eat your bread will set an ambush for you."*

Enter the Nabateans; The Nabateans were caravan drivers, traders and merchants whom the Edomites trusted and traded with. They were their business partners. They were allowed access into the city, but they turned against the Edomites and overthrew them. By 100 A.D. the Edomites were entirely lost to history. The ancient and prosperous capital Petra not rediscovered until 1812 by a Swiss explorer, Johann Ludwig Burckhardt.

Lessons For Today

The Lord takes a VERY dim view of betrayal !!

- The ultimate sin of Edom was its lack of family values or brotherliness. Edom stood by and gloated over the misfortune of a brother nation. "He who rejoices at calamity will not go unpunished" (Prov. 17:5).

- If you share in the spoils of wrong doing, even by 'standing aloof' you have become 'as one of them' (Ob 11).

- As you sow so will you reap – The Edomites sought to utterly destroy the Israelites but were themselves totally destroyed. (Obadiah 15). "Do not be deceived, God is not mocked; for whatever a man sows, this he will also reap!" (Gal. 6:7).

Pride comes before a fall, The Edomites were proud and arrogant . Read 2-4
Proverbs 16:18 "Pride *goes* before destruction, And a haughty spirit before stumbling."

Pride is all about 'I '
Remember Pride was the sin of Lucifer **READ…Isaiah 14:13,14** where you will see the five I Will's of Lucifer *"But you said in your heart,*
*'**I will** ascend to heaven;*
__I will__ raise my throne above the stars of God,
*And **I will** sit on the mount of assembly*
*In the recesses of the north. '**I will** ascend above the heights of the clouds;*
__I will__ make myself like the Most High. '

Daniel 4: 28-37 King Nebuchadnezzar ate grass for 7 years
Answer to pride – James 4:10 "Humble yourself before God and he will exalt you"

Often we ask ourselves the question, is this message from The Lord. Or perhaps is this individual for real ! So-called men and women of God will sometimes come up to you with a prophecy or a 'word from The Lord'. The bible tells us to judge every word to be sure of its origin and its validity, for false teachers will surely mingle amongst God's people.
 2 Peter 2:1-3 *But false prophets also arose among the people, just as there will also be false teachers among you, who will secretly introduce destructive heresies,*

even denying the Master who bought them, bringing swift destruction upon themselves. ² Many will follow their sensuality, and because of them the way of the truth will be maligned; ³ and in their greed they will exploit you with false words; their judgment from long ago is not idle, and their destruction is not asleep.

One of the surest ways to judge whether a message is from The Lord or not, is to look at the individual giving the message. Notwithstanding the fact that the Lord does indeed use 'broken vessels' to perform his purposes, a truly 'spiritual' individual will always display a certain humility or fear of The Lord in their lives and attitude.

The real signs of a Godly man or woman is not pride and arrogance but a Godly humility.

Summary

The conflict between Edom and Israel is often used to visualize the battle that goes on in a Christians life between the forces of evil (Edom) and the power of the Holy Spirit (Israel) in our lives.

The Apostle Paul , speaks about the fight between the flesh and the spirit that battles constantly within us (cf. Galatians 5:16–18 : Rom 7;24)
For the Christian, the fight against 'the flesh' or worldly desires goes on; **it does not stop** when you accept Jesus into your life.

The war against sin has already been won at the cross –
but the battle against the flesh continues and will
continue, until we finally meet with The Lord in
Heaven.

SPOTLIGHT ON THE MINOR PROPHETS

PROPHETS

Book 3

Joel

Part 3 of a Christian home-group discussion course on the 12 Prophets

James Paris

Book 3: JOEL

"Blow a trumpet on Zion, and sound an alarm on my Holy mountain! Let all the inhabitants of the land tremble, for the Day of The Lord is coming; surely it is near." Joel 2.2

Historical Setting.

The year is approx 830 B.C .
Judah is ruled by the boy King Joash (7 years old) .
When Prince Joash was just a baby, his father King Ahaziah was embroiled in a coup in neighboring Israel, and was killed. Immediately his mother (who took the title Queen Mother) Athaliah (daughter of Ahab & Jezebel) seized the throne herself, killing all her own male descendants as rivals. Baby Joash – the last remaining from the line of David - however, was rescued by the late king's sister, Joash's aunt Jehosheba. The wife of the Lord's Priest Jehoiada, she hid him in the temple, and the two of them raised him up.

When Joash was only 7 years old the priest Jehoiada overthrew Athaliah and placed Joash (the Lords choice) on the throne.
Tutored by the Godly priest Jehoiada, Joash started off well, but as is so often the case, ended up badly.

After the death of his mentor Jehoiada (at 130years old!) he could not cope with the pressure of his peers and abandoned the lord.

Joash finally commits murder by sentencing Jehoiada's son Zechariah (whom the Lord had sent to reason with him) to death.
Over 800 years later, Jesus later referred to this martyrdom when he said, *"From the blood of Abel unto the blood of Zacharias, which perished between the altar and the temple: verily I say unto you, It shall be required of this generation."* (Luke 11:51)

He was himself finally murdered by a group of his opponents as he lay in bed recuperating from a lost battle with the Syrians.
Not buried with the Kings but instead was given a commoners grave. (2 Chron 24:23-27)

Where to read Joash's story: 2 Kings 11 - 12; 2 Chronicles 22:10; 24:23-27

The Book

What's in a name? Joel means "Yahweh is God"
YHWH (Yahweh) or (Jehovah) the 'Tetragrammaton' the unpronounceable name of God, personal name to the Israelites.
Main Theme – Impending Judgment !   "The day of the Lord" and the Final restoration of God's people.

'Day of the Lord' in three phases

First 'day of the Lord'.
Read 1 ; 1-7
Starts with a terrible plague of locusts which have afflicted Judah and compares this with the coming judgment. Pointing out that as bad as it seems, there is a lot worse to come. (1:1-13)

Second 'Day of the Lord'.
Read 2:1-3
Warns of a terrible conflict to come. Joel 2:1-11.
This could be the coming captivity by the Babylonians in 587 or the destruction of Jerusalem in 70 AD or the events in the 'End Days' or indeed all of the above!
God calls the people to repent and 'Rend their hearts and not their garments' (2:13).
'Yet even now' v12-13 Talk.

Restoration of the Nation 2:18-27 …v25 "then I will make up for you the years that the swarming locusts have eaten"

READ (Joel 2:28) "*And it will come about after this That I will pour out My Spirit on all mankind; And your sons and daughters will prophesy, Your old men will dream dreams, Your young men will see visions.*"

Also Acts 2:17 familiar words; spoken by Peter on the day of Pentecost after the Holy Spirit had fallen and the disciples all began speaking in 'tongues'

Third 'Day of the Lord'.
Read 2:30-31
Even up to this time there is still time for repentance v32- 'whoever calls upon the name of the Lord will be saved' again, a familiar scripture. Used by Paul in Romans 10:13.
Also 3:14 – even the valley of judgment is called the valley of decision!
Further proof that God is indeed 'slow to anger and abounding in loving-kindness' (2:13).
Millennial Reign ? 3:16-18 **Read**

Applications for Today

This is perhaps one of the most exciting of the Minor Prophets with regards to our times.
Out of Three 'Days of the Lord', two have already passed and the third is possibly just around the corner.
The 'Battle of Armageddon' the final conflict between the forces of Good and Evil before the millennial reign of Christ.
Read Acts 2:17-21

First lesson

There is a judgment day coming, when God will judge the nation of Judah for their backslidden ways.
As is the case of most of the Old Testament prophecies, this has a present and a future meaning for the peoples of the earth.

It often seems to us, that God is a bystander in times of crises and it was indeed the same with the ancients. However although The Lord may be 'slow to anger', he does get angry ! Judgment for sins is not optional – it is inevitable.

The call to 'rend your hearts, and not your garments' is simply a call for true repentance and not the sham repentance of the person caught with their 'hands in the money box'.

Second Lesson

The Lord is always ready to forgive, and forgiveness leads to restoration.

One of the most exciting and yet the most un-acted upon scriptures in my opinion is this.

"If we confess our sins, He is faithful and righteous to forgive us our sins and to cleanse us from all unrighteousness." 1 John 1:9

Too many Christians today walk around with a heavy baggage of guilt on their shoulders. Even knowing the forgiveness of the Lord, they continue to let Satan rob them of their future joys, by reminding them of their past evils.

The forgiveness of God knows no boundaries, and no limitations.

The fact is that if you have received Jesus into your life, then you are already blessed beyond measure and

forgiven your past sins completely. The Psalmist put it correctly when he said "As far as the east is from the west,
So far has He removed our transgressions from us."
Psalm 103:12

Why would the devil like to remind you just how much of a sinner you are ? The answer is simple; a guilt ridden Christian is about as much use as a chocolate fire-guard! If you are struggling under a burden if sin and guilt; then you are hardly likely to make an effective witness, for the gospel of Jesus Christ.
The devil cannot take away your salvation, however he can take away your effectiveness as a herald of the gospel of Jesus Christ - if you allow him to.

Over the years I have come up against many Christians struggling with depression, often linked to guilt because of something that they have done, or commonly something that has been done to them that has left them ashamed and fearful. Even in bible college the call was sometimes "thank God and Prozac, I'm ok now!" verging on blasphemy I know, but that's the truth of it. As tragic as these things are, or have been; the answer is to start believing the scriptures, repent of any wrong-doing or perceived wrong-doing, and move on with life. The old saying "confession is good for the soul" in this instance is true. Not confession before men, but before God the Father, through the Son Jesus.

Question:

Is there any sin that The Lord will not forgive a repentant Christian ?
Perhaps think or discuss the 'unforgivable sin' of blasphemy against the holy Spirit. Matt 12:31-32

Can a Christian commit this sin…. NO
This is a case where Jesus was accused of healing by the power of Beelzebub, when in fact it was by the power of the Holy Spirit. Hence they were blaspheming against the Holy Spirit – the unforgivable sin.

Anyone who has accepted Jesus into their lives, has also accepted The Father and the Holy Spirit and as a consequence received the forgiveness of the fullness of God.
Anyone who says that as a Christian you have or could commit the unforgivable sin – knows nothing about the forgiveness of The Lord – end off.

Time for prayer.
This would be a good time to offer prayer either as a group or to individuals in a group, who have perhaps been struggling in this area of forgiveness.

Remember that to be effective ambassadors for the Gospel, then we all must be fully aware of the freedom from guilt that we have as born-again believers in the Gospel of Jesus Christ.

*****

SPOTLIGHT ON THE MINOR PROPHETS
PROPHETS
Book 4

Hosea

Part 4 of a Christian home-group discussion course on the 12 Prophets

James Paris

Book 4: HOSEA

Historical Setting.

The year is around 750 BC.
Israel is under the rule of Jeroboam 11 and later Pekah depending on actual date. Six Kings ruled during the last tragic 25 years of Israel. Although peace and apparent prosperity reigns, Judgement and chaos are just around the corner.

During Hosea's lifetime Kings priests and all their Aristocratic supporters had abandoned the ways of The Lord and instead followed the idolatrous ways of the Canaanites.

Religion was booming – but it was the religion of the fertility cults involving all kinds of sexual excess and perversion. **Power and Passion – the two greatest enemies of our relationship with God.**

Assyria looms as the executor of The Lords Judgement on a rebellious and adulterous Nation. In 733, just 17 years after this writing Israel was broken up by the Assyrians then in 722 their capital Samaria was captured and Israel was no more.

The Book

What's in a name?   Hosea means 'Salvation' and this is what the Lord offered to Israel if they would turn from their idolatry or adultery.

Main Theme: This book is all about RELATIONSHIP – God's relationship with his people which is falling apart owing to their adulterous behaviour. (Expand later)

Hosea can basically be split into two parts; 1st part chapters 1-3: 2nd part chapters 4-14.

First part READ 1;1-9

He is instructed to marry a Harlot named Gomer with whom he fathers 3 children, two sons and a daughter. The Lord names them.

The first child-a son- is named Jezreel meaning 'God Scatters'

Second child, a daughter named 'Lo-ruhamah' meaning 'Unloved' or 'Not Pitied'

Third child a boy named 'Lo-ammi' meaning 'Not my people' or 'not mine' he is understood to be a 'bastard' son.

This is pure theatre! The Lord is here showing Israel in the most graphic way, a way that they would understand, just what he thinks of their behaviour. He is impressing upon them that they have not only disobeyed his direct commands not to get involved with foreign gods etc but that they have broken their' marriage vows' in effect they have 'run off' and played the field.

Chapter 3 sees Hosea instructed to 'love a woman' who is also an adulteress (probably Gomer again) but not to be intimate with her for a number of days to symbolise the time that Israel would be without a King before they repented of their ways and returned to The Lord – who had been loyal and faithful.

Chapter 4 onwards really just spells out the whole allegory in more detail, pointing out Israel's unfaithfulness, the destructive path they are on and The Lords willingness to accept them back to Him and forgive them.

Applications for Today

Relationship!!!!

God wants it – We need it !

The Lord was angry with the Israelites why? Because they were committing adultery!

They had broken the marriage covenant and God was determined to bring them back into relationship READ Hosea 2:16. "It will come about in that day," declares the LORD THAT you will call Me Ishi, and will no longer call Me Baali.

(Ishi = "My Husband" , Baali = "My Master")
Jeremiah 3:20

Bring it Back.........Why is this relevant to us as Christians? For one – the 'Church' or 'believers' are frequently referred to as Christ's 'Bride' (2 Cor 11:2) (Eph 5:22-27).

God desires us to know him not just know about him, this is Relationship and in this relationship lies all the promises and power of Almighty God.

Question - Salvation , what is it? We are saved from hell, yes. We have an entrance visa for Heaven, Yes – however, John 3:16 "For God so loved the world..........eternal life"

 READ John 17:3 "This is eternal life, that they may know You, the only true God, and Jesus Christ whom You have sent"

The secret is in the word "Know" this is the same word 'ginosko' that we find in John 14:20- Read. "In that day you will <u>know</u> that I am in My Father, and you in Me, and I in you."
This goes way beyond a mental knowledge where we can know all **about** Him but not KNOW Him.

Relationships take time and effort (Talk on this area. Perhaps relate your own experiences on what relationship actually means – good times, and not so good times!)

Only through building a deep relationship with God the Father can we have any lasting effect on the world around us.
We can be well saved and live a life of charitable giving, feeding the poor, dish out tracts, knock on doors – all good works but totally meaningless if we do not have the love of God in our hearts. The Apostle Paul says that Without this love we and all our deeds are nothing (cf 1Cor 13).
(1 John 4:8) God is love (READ) "The one who does not love is not from God for God is love"

An Important Lesson

My own struggle – I was once assured that if I had no real love for the people, The Lord could not use me in Christian work. However after much prayer and seeking on my part, God led me to the prophet Jonah. He had no love for the Ninevites, in fact he wanted The Lord to destroy them utterly! Yet God used Jonah to bring salvation to the whole city.

The love of God in an individual can be shown in many ways, quite apart from the emotional love that we can all feel at times. Jonah was able to bring the love of God to the Ninevites even though he himself felt no love for them. Of course it is good if you can relate well to the people that you are bringing the good news of the gospel to; if you have a real love in your hearts for them then that is even better. However do not think for an instant that if you do not 'feel' anything, God cannot use you. Remember you are bringing the **Love of God** into a situation, through your own presence and willingness to perform His will.

What The Lord revealed to me was this; I have to work on my own relationship with God and through that will come an outpouring of love – "He that believeth on me, as the scripture hath said, out of his belly shall flow rivers of living water." (Jn 7:38).

Salvation – believing in Jesus – is just the beginning of our walk in the Lord; the real joy, fulfilment and power of New Testament Christianity lies in our own personal relationship.

We are all a work in progress – but how we progress is up to us!

HOSEA: PART 4b

Relationship Again!

Relationship is achieved when knowledge goes from the Head to the Heart.

I.E. The object of bible study is to discover more 'about' the Lord, to accumulate 'head' knowledge that we must then transfer to the 'heart'- the Spirit bearing witness – thereby truly getting to know The Lord on a much deeper personal level.

Question: So how do we transfer this knowledge from Head to Heart?

First of all we have to look at the three aspects of the human individual; what they are and what they represent in our lives.

Body, Soul and Spirit - Breakdown

Soul:

This is the 5 Senses – see, hear, touch, smell and taste. It is also the seat of our emotions, imaginations, values etc.

Regarding the supernatural things of God, the **Soul** is critical and unbelieving, as a result of the Fall from grace in the garden of Eden.

Spirit:

This is in fact the part of us that has been re-born. Upon salvation our own spirit was completely changed,

Sanctified, Justified, Purified in fact 'Born Again' "Christ in you the hope of glory" (Colossians 1:27). Regarding the supernatural things of God, His Spirit in us believes 100% !
Body:
The body is basically a slave to our other two parts, Here's the thing: whichever part of us (soul or spirit) has the upper hand will determine just how the body will react.

The Battle For Supremacy

There is a battle going on constantly between the Soul and the Spirit for dominance over the Body – if there is not, then there should be !
Paul describes this conflict in **Romans 7**. Where he describes in great (if somewhat confusing!) detail, the struggle between the body and the Spirit in his own life. Personally I have always found it something of a comfort that if a 'spiritual giant' such as the Apostle Paul should struggle with such things – then it is no surprise that we all should struggle at times.
In **Romans 12:2** he tells us about "Renewing our mind" what does this mean exactly? In its simplest form it means to listen to the Spirit within, rather than the Carnal voice of the Soul – which is corrupt and against the things of God.
Galatians ch5:16,17"But I say, walk by the Spirit, and you will not carry out the desire of the flesh. For the flesh sets its desire against the Spirit, and the Spirit against the flesh"

"If any man is in Christ he is a new creation, old things have passed away – behold, all things have become new" **(2 Cor 5:17)**.

Our body is still the same. If I had a wart on the end of my nose before I was saved, I will still have that wart after I've been saved! Our soul is still the same. I will still have the same carnal lusts and desires as I had before I was saved (albeit they are suppressed by the on-going work of the Spirit in my heart) It is our Spirit that has become new and which now leads us to seek after the things of God because therein lies life eternal, freedom and victory! (2 Cor 3;17 "Now the **Lord is** the **Spirit**, and where the **Spirit** of the **Lord is**, there **is** liberty.")

Back to Question – How do we transfer this 'head' knowledge to the 'heart'?
Good news & bad news!

Bad news first – It takes time and effort on our part ! there are no short cuts to build a proper relationship. "he who seeks the Lord <u>with all his heart </u>shall find Him" **(Jer 29:13) Prov 3:6** "In all your ways acknowledge Him, And He will make your paths straight."

Good news – God has made the first move! (Talk or meditate on the things that The Lord has done in your own life, perhaps giving testimony of your own salvation experience?)

If we are Christians, we already have the same power that raised Christ from the dead living within us ! IMAGINE - The Lord himself has already taken our hand and led us onto the dance floor, the floor is the World, we let him take the lead and the dance is on !!

How do we know when we have 'transferred' from Head to Heart?

When John the Baptist sent his disciples to ask Jesus if he truly was the messiah they were waiting for Jesus said "go and report what you see, the BLIND RECEIVE SIGHT and the lame walk, the lepers are cleansed and the deaf hear, the dead are raised up, and the POOR HAVE THE GOSPEL PREACHED TO THEM." (Matthew 11).
Jesus said to his disciples "These signs will accompany those who have believed: in My name they will cast out demons, they will speak with new tongues; they will pick up serpents, and if they drink any deadly poison, it will not hurt them; they will lay hands on the sick, and they will recover."(Mark 16:17-18).

In other words we will not only 'talk the talk' but we will 'walk the walk'.

Summary

Do not ever be fooled by the suggestion that the Christian walk would be easy – it is not!

Even a basic study of the epistles will show you that adversity is awaiting you at every turn, as you attempt to share your faith to a largely unbelieving world. It was never easy for the early disciples and it will certainly be no easier for us.

You may or may not believe in the devil. I can only say that if you do not, then you are at an even greater disadvantage, because how can you prepare to fight something that you do not believe exists! The Bible makes it clear "Be of sober spirit, be on the alert. Your adversary, the devil, prowls around like a roaring lion, seeking someone to devour." (1 Peter 5:8)

For all our 'advances' since these times of the early disciples, the battle between the forces of good and evil are the same as they ever were, its just the surroundings that have changed.

As mentioned at the beginning of this work; Hosea is all about relationship, and in particular our relationship with The Lord. If we get this right, and make Him the focus of our lives, then we are indeed putting on the 'full armour' that we see in the book of Ephesians (Eph:6;10).

*****

SPOTLIGHT ON THE MINOR PROPHETS

PROPHETS

Book 5

Amos

*Part 5 of a Christian home-group
discussion course on the 12 Prophets*

James Paris

Book 5: AMOS

Historical Setting:

The year is around 760-755 BC.
Israel is under the Kingship of Jeroboam 11 who died 753 BC.
Judah's King at this time is Uzziah.
Amos is a contemporary of the prophet Hosea and so the social and religious problems that Hosea faced were the same.

As with Hosea, Amos preached against the social and moral decline of Israel. The worship of Assyrian deities and the huge gulf that had emerged between the 'haves' and the 'have not's '
Assyria and Damascus had been at one another's throats for some years now and so Israel was 'allowed' to prosper in a material sense. They had winter houses and summer houses, houses of Ivory (Amos 3:15).
Houses of 'hewn stone' (5:11) and they reclined on "Beds of Ivory" (6:4)
They were "at ease in Zion" (6:1)
As in the book of Hosea "Religion" was prospering but Faith in the one true God YHWH was on the decline.

Along comes a farmer called Amos! Not one of the recognized prophets of Israel, nor was he a priest, not even a native of Israel but a farmer called of the Lord

from Judah to warn the Northern Kingdom of the coming judgement.
Read Amos: 1:5 – 7:4-16

THE BOOK

What's in a name? Amos means 'Burden bearer'.

Main Theme Ch5:24 Justice and righteousness

In the first two chapters there are eight condemnations introduced by the words " For three transgressions and for four" What's that all about ?
This was to empathise that the Lord was entitled to judge Israel on the basis of not just three transgressions;

but four. This pointed to the severity of the crime and the coming judgement.

Read Amos 1:3

Two or Three witnesses were required if a crime worthy of death was to be judged –

READ Deuteronomy 17:6

Four signifies the absolute completeness of the testimony. (The Lord is slow to anger, abounding in loving-kindness)
The message of Amos however is not only aimed at Israel and Judah but includes her immediate neighbours as we see from the 'For the three transgressions and for four' Damascus, Gaza, Tyre, Edom, Ammon and Moab are all included in the Judgement but special emphasis is upon Judah and Israel because they should have known better! – they knew God but rebelled.

As Hosea's main theme was Israel's Adultery against the Lord and therefore about broken relationship; the message of Amos was predominantly about Israel's social corruption and moral decline.

Amos was an 'unwelcome southerner' as far as the priests of Israel were concerned and Amaziah rushed to report him to King Jeroboam hoping to get him kicked out of the country.

READ 7:10-17

Message of Hope

Amos ends with a message of hope. **Read Amos 9:11-15**

11 *"In that day I will raise up the fallen booth of David,*
And wall up its breaches;
I will also raise up its ruins
And rebuild it as in the days of old;
12 *That they may possess the remnant of Edom*
And all the nations who are called by My name,"
Declares the Lord who does this.
13 *"Behold, days are coming,"* *declares the Lord,*
"When the plowman will overtake the reaper
And the treader of grapes him who sows seed;
When the mountains will drip sweet wine
And all the hills will be dissolved.

¹⁴ "Also I will restore the captivity of My people Israel,
And they will rebuild the ruined cities and live in them;
They will also plant vineyards and drink their wine,
And make gardens and eat their fruit.
¹⁵ "I will also plant them on their land,
And they will not again be rooted out from their land
Which I have given them,"
Says the Lord your God.

 After a whole catalogue of denunciations from the prophet Amos, he comes up with 5 great promises to the people of Israel from the Lord Almighty. Theses promises are of great blessing and restoration for God's people, put in the following terms.

- **The re-building of Israel:** After the separation of Israel following the death of King Solomon, and the subsequent capture and destruction of both nations. God now promises that the day will come when both nations will be restored again as one nation under his rule and the rule of the house of David. This happened in the days of Ezra and Nehemiah when the people returned from exile and re-built the city of Jerusalem.

- **Victory over enemies:** As we have seen the Edomites were old enemies of Israel, and took advantage of them whenever they could. The Lord promises there will come a day when they would have victory over their enemies.

- **Abundance:** There is to come a time of great abundance, when the grapes will grow faster than they can pick them. A time of great prosperity is near at hand.

- **Security:** A time of security when they can enjoy the fruits of their labours, instead of living in fear of their enemies.

- **Lasting Inheritance:** The final verse talks about a time when they will be gathered together as a nation, never again to be dispersed. Many would say that this occurred in 1948 when Israel again became a nation after being dispersed for almost 2,000 years. This was a momentous occasion and the first time in history that any peoples have ever been restored after such a long passage of time.

Applications for Today

Prosperity can be both a blessing and a curse, and the behaviour of the privileged in Israel emphasised this problem.

The 'upper classes' of Israel had never had it so good. They had second homes in the country, houses adorned with Ivory, Stone built houses with all the mod cons (a total luxury) slaves, concubines etc, they lacked for nothing and yet as the Lord had to point out through his servant Amos – they were Morally and Spiritually bankrupt.

This is a pattern that seems to apply to all the major world Empires or Kingdoms throughout history. Along with prosperity comes increasing corruption and lawlessness, eventually leading to their downfall.

Things have not changed today. Our western civilisation is by any standards of measure living in a time of great prosperity; and just as in the time of Amos it is very unevenly distributed; but this is exactly what Amos was ranting about – the rich get richer while the poor suffer. Charity is hard to find and instead the wealthy are oppressing and taking advantage of the poor.

More and more the laws that God has set up are being ignored and instead the masses are persuaded to worship 'mammon' Wealth for Wealth's sake and it doesn't matter who you tread on to get it.

God wants us to prosper (Psalm 1-3), yes; but at any cost?

The trouble with prosperity is that it is too easy to lose sight of the provider – as we look wide eyed at the provision !
We tend to really seek God when we need him to provide for our needs, but then when that provision is met and we are 'comfortable' do we still seek the presence of the Lord with as much gusto ?

Conclusion:

It is right and just to as the Lord to meet our every need whether it be Health, Wealth or even relationships, however we must be careful not to let the **Provision** take the place of the **Provider.** And especially not to allow our **prosperity** to outweigh our **charity!**
It is all too easy when we are facing trials of whatever nature, to turn to God in desperate prayer. However when life is good and things are progressing well; it is just as easy to forget to pray at all.
The Christian life is all about keeping the correct balance between Worship and Wealth – or lack of it!

Question for the group:

When is your relationship, or worship time with the Lord at its strongest – when you're in need, or when you have plenty?

*****

Book 6: MICAH

Historical Setting.

The period is approx 770-710 B.C . although it is
generally thought that the book was written just before
the fall and destruction of Samaria (the capital of the
northern kingdom of Israel) by the Assyrians in 721.
During this time Judah is ruled in turn by a series of
kings. Jotham, Ahaz and Hezekiah.
Read Ch1v1
This is also confirmed in Jeremiah 26:17 "…..Micah of
Moresheth prophesied during the days of Hezekiah
king of Judah"
It is during this period that we see the rise of Assyria as
a major world player under the kingship of Tiglath-
Pileser 111 (745-727bc) one of the most successful
military commanders in world history - and an
impending threat to the kingdoms of Israel and Judah.

Micah's Ministry

What's in a name? Micah means "Who is like unto
the Lord"
Little is known about the personal life of Micah, though
it is generally thought that he was a man of the soil, and
closely connected to the common people – a farmer
perhaps. We know that he was from Moresheth in the
southern kingdom of Judah (about 25 miles from

Jerusalem) and it's worth noting that he was indeed a contemporary of the prophets Isaiah, Amos and Hosea.

As is the way of most of the 'minor' prophets, Micah spoke out about the injustice he seen around him. This was a time when the wealthy landowners were growing richer by bribing corrupt judges to fix land deeds in their favour, thereby putting the smaller landowners out of business. The peasants and the landless of course suffered the most during this time.

Read Ch2:1-3.....7:2-3
This in turn led to an overcrowding in the cities as the small farmers looked for employment elsewhere.
Along with this practice there was a general move away from the worship of the true God and the corruption of the covenants he had set aside for them to follow.
The country was being led by corrupt leaders as is emphasised in Ch2:11 *"If a man walking after wind and falsehood had told lies and said 'I will speak out to you concerning wine and liquor' He would be spokesman to this people"*
The Lord was saying here- none to subtly- that they were being led by a bunch of lying, thieving drunkards !

The worship of Baal and other pagan deities added to the general backslidden state of the nation. It is in this light that we see the foretold destruction of Samaria- one of the leaders of the conspiracy- in Ch1:2-15.

Both Amos and Hosea had tackled the same questions in the Northern Kingdom. Their answer had been that the Northern Kingdom would not survive. By the time Micah began his ministry, Isaiah of Jerusalem had already been addressing the same questions for 20 years. The Northern Kingdom had already been destroyed, or would be in a matter of months. And as both prophets looked at the Southern Kingdom of Judah, they saw much the same conditions as had existed in the Northern Kingdom.

Judah's future was not certain. But both Isaiah and Micah consistently proclaimed that a change, a return to faithfulness to God, was essential if the Southern Kingdom was to have any future.

This is a hope borne out by these passages referring to a coming saviour and redemption. **Ch4:1-7** and **Ch7:7-8** *"But as for me I will watch expectantly for the Lord; I will wait for the God of my salvation. My God will hear me. 8. Do not rejoice over me O my enemy. Though I fall I will rise; though I dwell in darkness the Lord is a light for me."*

Applications for Today

Main lesson – The Lord God hates injustice, corruption, false dealing as much as he hates the worship of false idols and the manipulation of his statutes and laws to suit our own ends !
The leaders of Micah's time were doing just that, they twisted the laws of the land to suit themselves, and no doubt called it piety !
Jesus condemned the same attitude in the Pharisees – the religious leaders of his time.

This is a classic example to us that all things must be taken not only on 'face value' but according to the context in which they are written.
I could start a new cult tomorrow – Jims apostles and latter day saints- and easily use the Bible to back it up!
How ? I simply decide what I would like out of my personal cult and then look up all the passages I can find to support my cause – ignoring along the way the context in which they are written and of course all the passages against it.

I might even get a reprint of the bible with some subtly altered passages, endorsed by a corrupt translator who is quite happy to lend his name to it for the parting of some cash !

Lets call it 'The New World Truth Bible'

Throughout history, right up to modern times numerous cults, movements and sects have mis-quoted scripture in order to justify their particular actions. Che Guevara the Marxist revolutionary quoted scripture when it suited the cause; and Charismatic preachers like Jim Jones or David Koresh are just two examples of how the Scriptures can be corrupted to suit evil means. Both Mussolini and Adolph Hitler claimed at various times to be Christian; Hitler promoting his 'positive christianity' which was the Nazi ideal of a Christianity without Jews or any other undesirables, and which was infused with Nazi doctrines.

The Word of God must be 'correctly divined' as they used to say. We cannot quote *Wives, submit to your husbands as to the Lord.* without reading the whole chapter which includes -

Husbands, love your wives, just as Christ loved the church and gave himself up for her. **EPH 5**

The leaders of Israel and Judah had grown complacent and corrupt. They had forgotten that they were dealing with a living God who sees all and who will demand recompense.

While we have of course a New Covenant and are Justified not by our own works but by the sacrifice of

Jesus on the Cross we are nevertheless still called on to *'do justice, to love kindness, and to walk humbly before our God'* **Ch6:8**

The inherent danger of any society in any age is that power drifts into the hands of corrupt people, who will use this power and influence not for the common good – but to line their own pockets.
The old adage that 'power corrupts, and absolute power corrupts absolutely' is as applicable now as it has been throughout the centuries from the beginning of time. There is indeed - as the preacher says in the book of Ecclesiastes – nothing new under the sun, and corruption is as prevalent now as it ever was. It is also true that "all it needs for evil to succeed, is for good people to stand by and do nothing while it is happening."

Question:
Micah spoke out against the corruption in high places that he witnessed in his time – what examples do you see before you in the times in which we live?

*****

Nahum

*Part 7 of a Christian home-group
Discussion course on the 12 Prophets*

James Paris

Book 7: NAHUM

Historic Introduction

The year is <u>around</u> 655 BC and the Assyrian empire is on the rampage under the leadership of King Ashurbanipal.

Exact date is hard to fix but strong evidence is supplied by Nahum 3:8 **READ** *"Are you better than Thebes, situated on the Nile, with water around her? the river was her defence, the waters her wall"*.

This means that the city of Thebes had already succumbed to the Assyrian onslaught, at the time of Nahum's writing.

No-Amon = the Egyptian city of Thebes destroyed 663 bc by the Assyrians themselves.

The northern kingdom of Israel had already succumbed to the forces of Assyria in 722 BC when Samaria their capital city fell.

Assyrians "conquer and divide."

The Assyrian way of dealing with captive nations was to divide them around the Empire, thereby reducing any chance of rebellion – this is where the 'ten lost tribes' were scattered never to be found again.

When the Babylonians conquered the southern kingdom over 100 years later, the occupants were located in one place in Babylon, where they set up the first synagogues and managed to retain their identity.

By this means The Lord assured that a 'remnant' would return, when all was well.

In 701 Sennacherib laid siege to Jerusalem. However just when things looked at their bleakest, and even Hezekiah himself was clothed in sackcloth and ashes; the Lord delivered them from their enemies resulting in the destruction of 185,000 Assyrian troops, and the eventual murder of Sennacherib in the temple of his gods by his own two sons. **Isaiah 37:38**

HEAVENLY WEATHER FORECAST

Judah, although still an independent state was in fact- notwithstanding the Grace of God- a vassal of Assyria. Manasseh was King at this time. The most evil King that Judah had known, he came to the throne after the good king Hezekiah and was so involved with the Assyrian gods that he burned his two sons to death as a sacrifice to the idol Molech.

He "filled Jerusalem from one end to the other" with innocent blood 2 Kings 21:16
Reigned 55 years.
Late in his kingship he repented truly of his deeds.

What's in a name?

Nahum can be translated to mean 'Consolation,' and the roll of Nahum does indeed seem to be that of a comforter to Israel, and the nations that Assyria had oppressed.

Very little is known for certain about Nahum, except that he came from Elkosh (1.1) and even then, we do not know where it was exactly.

READ Nahum 1:2-6
"A jealous and avenging God is the Lord;
The Lord is avenging and wrathful.
The Lord takes vengeance on His adversaries,
And He reserves wrath for His enemies.
³ The Lord is slow to anger and great in power,
And the Lord will by no means leave the guilty unpunished.
In whirlwind and storm is His way,
And clouds are the dust beneath His feet.
⁴ He rebukes the sea and makes it dry;
He dries up all the rivers.
Bashan and Carmel wither;
The blossoms of Lebanon wither.
⁵ Mountains quake because of Him
And the hills dissolve;

Indeed the earth is upheaved by His presence,
The world and all the inhabitants in it.
⁶ Who can stand before His indignation?
Who can endure the burning of His anger?
His wrath is poured out like fire
And the rocks are broken up by Him."

The book itself concentrates on the coming judgement
of Nineveh by an angry God !! Including the
destruction if the city itself and the futility of trying to
avoid or avert this judgement.

Questions

1.- Why was God angry?
God is not mocked – Galatians 6:7 *"Do* not *be*
deceived, God is not mocked; *for whatever a man sows,*
this he will also reap"
The Assyrians (Ninevites) that The Lord had forgiven
some 100 years ago, (Think of the warnings given
through the Prophet Jonah) have resorted to their old
ways – in fact they had started to 'backslide' shortly
after the ascendancy of Tiglath Pileser 111 in 745 **BC**
around 20 years after Jonah's preach.
In effect they 'repented of their repentance' – 2 Peter
2:22 'pig returns to wallowing in the mire' …..False
repentance.

2. – What did he do about it ?
First of all he sent his prophets, to warn of coming
judgement i.e. Nahum, Zephaniah (2:13) Isaiah etc.

Nahum prophesises the fall of Nineveh – inconceivable at the time as it was reputed to be impregnable.

There was however an old Ninevan prophecy that said the 'City would not be taken until the river became an enemy……….'

During a siege by the Babylonian forces in 614BC the river rose and destroyed a large section of the wall……….

King Esarhaddon 11 on hearing of the breach fled to the palace with his entire harem, his eunuch and all the treasures he could carry and burned them all to the ground!

Nahum 1:8, 2:6 **Read**

Nineveh the great city is captured and destroyed utterly – lost in the sands until its re-discovery in 1842.

Lessons/Applications for today

1. Don't mess with an angry God.

Fairly obvious – a no-brainer! When he moves in judgement nothing escapes.

2. God is slow to anger – but complete in its execution!
3. Don't get him angry to begin with.
One of the ways to avoid this is to 'let your yes be yes and your no be no' …James 5:12.
1 Peter 6:5 "God is opposed to the proud, but gives Grace to the humble"

HEAVENLY WEATHER FORECAST

As Christians –followers of Christ, we are told to be examples to the rest of the world. We are the 'salt of the world'…. Ambassadors for Christ.
3. Question … Does God get angry with Christians?
Hmmmmm….. NO! with qualifications (Discuss)
John 3:36 "he who has the Son has life……"
Romans 5:8-11 Read
BUT…. Hebrews 12:6 "those whom the Lord loves he disciplines"
TALK – Discipline of a loving father rather that an angry God.
Hebrews 12:11 Read
"All discipline for the moment seems not to be joyful, but sorrowful; yet to those who have been trained by it, afterwards it yields the peaceful fruit of righteousness.

Whilst we escape the wrath and judgement of an angry God we are nevertheless liable to his discipline."

Summary.

Nineveh faced the Wrath of an angry God and were destroyed utterly. *(The mills of God……) Nineveh sowed the wind of destruction – they must now reap the whirlwind of God's wrath and judgement !*
Christians face the chastisement of a Loving God and are renewed completely.
(2 Cor 5:17) *"if any man is in Christ all things have passed away, behold all things have become new"*

*****

SPOTLIGHT ON THE MINOR PROPHETS
PROPHETS
Book 8

Zephaniah

R_1 – REBELLION
R_2 – RETRIBUTION
R_3 – REPENTANCE
R_4 – RESTORATION

Part 8 of a Christian home-group
Discussion course on the 12 Prophets

James Paris

Book 8: ZEPHANIAH
Historic info / background

Zephaniah (Contemporary of Jeremiah) preached around 625 bc - King Manasseh is dead after a reign of 55 years – the most evil King in Judah he was the exact opposite of his father King Hezekiah.

Manasseh's son Amon is also dead after a reign of only 2 years he was assassinated by his own servants.

We are now in the reign of 'good' King **Josiah..** 640-609 who took the throne at the ripe old age of 8 years!

Age of Josiah's reforms

Final countdown – Only 11 years to the destruction of Nineveh in 614; under 40 years to the loss of Jerusalem to the Babylonians in 586.

Whole region in turmoil .. Assyria on the back foot with the rise of the Medio Persians and Babylonians......Judah on the edge of massive reform under Josiah.

A time of huge spiritual and political upheaval.

Josiah met his death whilst trying to hinder the Pharaoh Neco 11 from lending aid to Assyrian forces at Harran. Succeeded by Jehoahaz – who was deposed by Pharaoh – the first king of Judah to die in exile.

Where to read Josiah's story: 2 Kings 22:1 - 23:30; 2 Chronicles 34:1 - 35:27

The Book

Needless to say…..BOOK OF JUDGEMENT !
"Day of the Lord" mentioned **17 times** between 1:7 –
2:3.

George Adam Smith, in The Book of the Twelve
Prophets; *"No hotter book lies in all the Old
Testament. Neither dew nor grass nor tree nor any
blossom lives in it, but it is everywhere fire, smoke and
darkness, drifting chaff, ruins, nettles, salt pits, and
owls and raven looking from the windows of desolate
palaces."*

**Some would say that the happiest thing about this
book is the fact that it is only 3 chapters !!!**

However they would be wrong! Read 3:14-17

*"Shout for joy, O daughter of Zion!
Shout in triumph, O Israel!
Rejoice and exult with all your heart,
O daughter of Jerusalem!
15 The Lord has taken away His judgments against you,
He has cleared away your enemies.
The King of Israel, the Lord, is in your midst;
You will fear disaster no more.
16 In that day it will be said to Jerusalem:
" Do not be afraid, O Zion;
Do not let your hands fall limp.*

¹⁷ *"The Lord your God is in your midst,*
A victorious warrior.
He will exult over you with joy,
He will be quiet in His love,
He will rejoice over you with shouts of joy."

The book of Zephaniah follows the pattern of the Four R's Rebellion, Retribution, Repentance, Restoration. So often found in the teachings of the prophets of Israel.

1. **Rebellion:** The people rebel against the teachings of the Lord or his servants the Prophets.
2. **Retribution:** The Lord exacts retribution or judgement against them.

3. **Repentance:** The people see the error of their ways – leading to repentance, or a 'turning away' from evil.
4. **Restoration:** When the people finally see the error of their ways and repent, then The Lord is able (and willing) to restore fully.

The Lords judgement is not about him 'getting his own back' ! It is about bringing people to **repentance** so that he is able to **restore** or forgive.

What's in a name?....Zephaniah, who's name means 'the Lord Hides – or conceals.'

King Hezekiah was his great great grandfather and so of royal blood, during the reign of Manasseh all royal descendants were destroyed to secure his own position; he even sacrificed his own son top the pagan god Molech (2 kings 16) burning him alive.

Zephaniah however, The Lord concealed until the time was ripe.

This book warns the people of a comprehensive judgement not only on Assyria-the old enemy- but also on all the nations surrounding Judah and ultimately on Judah itself !

Judgement on the nations East and West

Zeph 2:4-7 Philistia.

Zeph 2:8-11 Moab & Amon.

Judgement on nations South and North

Zeph 2:12 Ethiopia. "You also Ethiopians will be slain by the sword"

Zeph 2:13-15 Assyria …**READ**

"And He will stretch out His hand against the north
And destroy Assyria,
And He will make Nineveh a desolation,
Parched like the wilderness.
14 Flocks will lie down in her midst,
All beasts which range in herds;
Both the pelican and the hedgehog
Will lodge in the tops of her pillars;
Birds will sing in the window,
Desolation will be on the threshold;
For He has laid bare the cedar work.
15 This is the exultant city
Which dwells securely,
Who says in her heart,
" I am, and there is no one besides me."
How she has become a desolation,

A resting place for beasts!
Everyone who passes by her will hiss
And wave his hand in contempt."

This was of course fulfilled completely in 614 B.C.
With the destruction of Nineveh the capital city of
Assyria.

Judgement on Jerusalem ......WHY ?
Zeph 3:1-4 **READ.....**2 Kings 24:3-4 *"Surely at the*
commandment of the LORD came this upon Judah, to
*remove them out of his sight, for the **sins of Manasseh**,*
*according to all that he did; And also for the **innocent***
blood that he shed**: for he **filled Jerusalem with
***innocent blood**; which the LORD would not pardon."*

Again, Judgement then repentance leads ultimately to
Blessing 3:14-17

Today's Relevance

Maybe more than you would think!
In the book of Zephaniah, we have the familiar lessons about the Lord's Judgement on Sin and Rebellion. It was fairly severe to say the least, making the God of the Old Testament <u>seem</u> to some like a very severe, stern task-master not to be crossed!

We are fortunate that as Christians we are able to 'approach the throne' so to speak, under an entirely different relationship with The Lord almighty. A relationship that has been made possible only through the sacrifice of Jesus, who is now our advocate or intercessor before God.

Some things however have not changed. The 'four r's' of Rebellion, Retribution, Repentance and Restoration; is still a pattern today for Christians when we rebel in any aspect of our everyday lives.
The scripture says that *"whom The Lord loves, he also chastises."* (Heb 12:6)

The main difference being; we have chastisement of a loving parent rather than an angry God?

Points for discussion..

- Is the God of the Old Testament really all 'smoke and thunder' – a God of wrath and judgement?
- What is the difference between our relationship with God, and the relationship that a common individual in the Old Testament times would have had?
- If we have already been forgiven through the sacrifice and blood of Christ – Is repentance still necessary!?

*****

Book 9: HABAKKUK

Historical Setting

Based around BC 610 after the fall of the Nineveh in 614, Habakkuk is the last of the Minor Prophets before the fall of Jerusalem to the Babylonian forces in BC 597.

Prophesied between the reigns of Josiah (died 609) and King Jehoahaz his successor.

Judah was in crises once more as the 'good' King Josiah was killed in battle with the Egyptians and Jehoahaz (the younger son) took up the reins of power. Unfortunately after only three months the Egyptians deposed him and removed him to Egypt, where he later died. He was replaced by the Egyptians with Jehoiakim; who once again led the nation down the slippery slope of idol worship by re-instating the temples and priests of Molech and Baal.

King Jehoiakim switched allegiances to the Babylonians after their victory over the Egyptians at the battle of Carchemish in 605 BC, however switched back again after only 3 years – bad move – this resulted in the siege and fall of Jerusalem to Nebuchadnezzar 11 of the Babylonians in 597 BC.

He was succeeded by his 18 year old son Jeconiah, who only reigned three months 10 days before being taken into captivity to Babylon, along with a number of other nobles and craftsmen.

Zedekiah is placed on the throne by the Nebuchadnezzar 11.
It is now only Ten years to the destruction of Jerusalem

THE BOOK

Main Focus of his message – Judgement-Again!

- The coming destruction by the Babylonians, on the rebellious people of Judah. (1:5-11)
- Judgement on the Surrounding nations. (1:4-18)
- Restoration of the remnant. (3:12,13)
- Remember 4 R's - Rebellion, retribution, repentance then restoration.

What's in a name? Habakkuk means to "he clings to" or "embraces".
Habakkuk has questions he needs answers to!!
Hab 1:1-4 **READ**
"The oracle which Habakkuk the prophet saw.
² How long, O Lord, will I call for help,
And You will not hear?
I cry out to You, "Violence!"
Yet You do not save.
³ Why do You make me see iniquity,

And cause me to look on wickedness?
Yes, destruction and violence are before me;
Strife exists and contention arises.
⁴ Therefore the law is ignored
And justice is never upheld.
For the wicked surround the righteous;
Therefore justice comes out perverted."

What makes Habakkuk unusual is that most prophesies God address's the people through the Prophets, but here Habakkuk addresses God directly – no other prophet starts this way.

Habakkuk even dares to question the plans of The Lord to use the Babylonians to administer judgement on Judah, admitting a little concern or confusion over God's plans.

(1:13)

We all know about **intercessory prayer** - Habakkuk gives us an example of **interrogatory prayer** – where we ask questions of God …..Why do the wicked prosper?

Example: 1:13-14

"Why are You silent when the wicked swallow up Those more righteous than they?
[14] Why have You made men like the fish of the sea, Like creeping things without a ruler over them?"

Sound Bites

One of the most quotable books, it is full of 'sound bites' that most of us would recognise i.e. **'The righteous will live by faith'** (2:4) the battle cry of the reformist movement. This was really picked up and carried along by Martin Luther, as he had sudden revelation from The Lord that it was faith and not works which counted as righteousness.

'The Lord is in his holy temple let all the earth be silent before him"(2:20)
Hab 1:5 "I am doing something in your days…….."

"Though the fig tree should not blossom……….."(3:17-18) READ
"Though the fig tree should not blossom
And there be no fruit on the vines,
Though the yield of the olive should fail
And the fields produce no food,
Though the flock should be cut off from the fold
And there be no cattle in the stalls,
[18] Yet I will exult in the Lord,
I will rejoice in the God of my salvation."

This particular passage was most relevant as the Babylonians were notorious for their 'scorched earth policy' when they went to war they left no living thing in their path – killed man and beast, destroyed crops on the way.
After the Babylonian armies had passed through a land, there was nothing left but despair – or your belief that God was indeed still on the throne.

Relevance for Today

Apart from a lot of great sound bites – Honesty!

An example of supreme honesty before God, pretence is NOT acceptable practice.

Most of us, if we are honest, sort of skirt around any questions we have regarding The Lords desires or purposes. Often we really do not feel that 'spiritual justice' has been done, and yet we do not dare to question God about it.

Habakkuk however had no such concerns – why? Because he knew more than anyone that The Lord reads the heart, more than he listens to your voice sometimes.

In other words, we cannot hide our real feelings or questions from The Lord – no matter how we may hide them from other people.

In fact, it could be said that to try and hide your true feelings from God, is to lie to Him – perish the thought!

Important point however – we **ask** questions of God – we do **NOT** question him!

Questioning God is closely linked to unbelief – asking questions simply acknowledge our own confusion in relation to what we know about our God – that he is Righteous!

Only he is omniscient – we cannot know everything.

He complains ……God answers…..worse is yet to come!! (ch1:6)

We may ask God things – sometimes we won't like the answer!

Most Important thing – God DID answer Habakkuk.

Discussion point for the group:

Even in your own quiet time, do you find it difficult to confess your own feelings or doubts before The Lord, and if so, why?

*****

SPOTLIGHT ON THE MINOR PROPHETS
Book 10

Haggai

BE STRONG AND WORK, FOR I AM WITH YOU, SAYS THE LORD OF HOSTS!

Part 10 of a Christian home-group discussion course on the 12 Prophets

James Paris

Book 10: HAGGAI

Historical Setting.

The period is approx 520 B.C. We know this date to be reasonably accurate as the Prophet dates his own work in the "second year of Darius the king." This is Darius I, son of Hystaspes (522-486 BC).
Seventy years earlier the kingdom of Judah had been conquered and taken into captivity by Nebuchadnezzar King of the Babylonian empire. They were forced to settle in Babylon in an area by the Chebar river.
This was to have a fundamental and long-term impact on the survival of the nation of Israel throughout the ages.

Judah's city's had been reduced to ruins and the whole kingdom laid waste. Some however were left to stay amongst the ruins and they were eventually joined by others who in turn fled the destruction of Babylon by Cyrus in 539.
This "collective of the dispossessed" would eventually become known as the Samaritans who would become a thorn in the flesh of the post exilic Israelites.
In 538 Cyrus issued a decree allowing the Jews to return to their homeland.

Over 150 years *before* this event, Isaiah had prophesied that God would use Cyrus to bring about this restoration (Isaiah 44:24 - 45:7).

Return in three stages

The actual return to the 'promised land' took place in three main stages.

1. The first group was in 536 when Haggai and Zechariah returned with approx 50,000 under the command of Zerubbabel. (Ezra 2.) It can be reasonably assumed that Haggai was a child upon his return.
2. The second group was not until 457 some 79 years later led by **Ezra** this was around 2058 people (Ezra 8-10).
3. The third and final group was 445 BC and led by Nehemiah who served as the governor of Jerusalem.

Why not all return at once?

It is easy to read the Bible and read the history of the return from exile, and at the same time not form any impression of the timescale involved.

The fact is however that between the first stage in 536 and the last stage in 445 BC; some 91 years had passed by! This meant that many of the so-called exiles were in fact citizens of Babylon, and knew next to nothing about Jerusalem apart from what they had been told by their parents and elders.

Businesses had been set up, Synagogues established and life - in what would be for some – in 'their' country, well set up. In other words, many of the Jews would not have much to gain and everything to lose by going back to a homeland still suffering from the ravages of Nebuchadnezzar, all these years ago.
All these doubts and fears had to be overcome before the people could feel confident enough to return.

The situation at the time of Haggai was this: After a good start upon their return in 536 work on the temple had ceased for the previous 16 years or so. The people had become obsessed by their own security and personal comfort, in the most part brought about by the influence of the Samaritans; who because the Jews would allow them no part in the rebuilding of the Temple, did their best to obstruct them at every turn. Apathy towards the building of the new Temple was rife. **1:2 - Thus says the LORD of hosts, 'This people**

says, "**The time has not come, even the time for the house of the LORD to be rebuilt.**"

The people were disillusioned, discouraged and generally lacking the motivation to carry on with the task they had begun. Beset on all sides by opposition in one form or another, the building program had come to a standstill.

Enter Haggai.....

THE BOOK

What's in a name? Haggai means "Festival or Festive or My Feast"

Main Theme ....Build the Temple!

Haggai was what we might call today a 'one trick pony' He was unashamedly single minded in doing the one thing that the Lord had called him to, and that was to get the building program re-started.

Haggai was a motivator, someone who could get 'the show back on the road', and point the people to the real important issue – their relationship with The Lord

In this he was VERY successful and the 'secret' to his success lay in just one thing – his dependence on the Word of the Lord.

26 times in a book of only 38 verses he quotes God as the Divine source and the inspiration of his messages; **'say's the Lord of Hosts'** and **'declares The Lord'** amongst others, are used to re-enforce the message and to give it absolute authority.

The people responded to this message because they recognised The Lord was indeed behind it.

Psalm 127:1- "Unless the LORD builds the house, they labour in vain who build it;

Unless the LORD guards the city, The watchman keeps awake in vain."

In 516 BC After just 4 years of haranguing by Haggai the Temple was rebuilt. Twenty years after it was first started and seventy years after it was destroyed by the Babylonians.

Applications for Today

Main lesson – Faithfullness to the call of The Lord.

Haggai had a calling on his life, and he was true to that calling and placed it above all other considerations. He was single minded in his objective which was of course to build the temple.

The Lord rewarded this loyalty with real success and Haggai is regarded as one of the most successful of the Prophets – perhaps only Jonah could claim equal response with his message against Nineveh.

The real basis for successful preaching is 'Thus saith the Lord' in other words when God is behind our message and we are faithfull to deliver it, notwithstanding all the opposition that may come our way; then a positive result is guarenteed.

Haggai would encourage us to look at what is really important – our own relationship with The Lord. It is only by having a close personal relationship with our saviour, that we can know just what his calling on our life is; not just in general terms, but indeed in exact terms – just like Haggai.

It is all too easy to get discouraged in life, whether it is in our walk with The Lord, or indeed in our workplace. The fact is that sometimes we lack motivation to carry on, to 'fight the good fight' or 'run the race' as the Apostle Paul would put it. (2 Tim:4-7)

These are the times when The Lord will put people in our path, who will motivate and encourage us to continue and believe against the odds sometimes, that he does indeed have a plan for our lives.

Jeremiah 29:11 *"For I know the plans that I have for you,'
declares the* LORD, *'plans for welfare and not for
calamity to give you a future and a hope."*

Or perhaps it is **YOU** that God has sent out to do the
motivating...

**Question 1: Do you know the Lord's plan for your
life?**
Question 2: What do you intend to do about it?

*****

SPOTLIGHT ON THE MINOR PROPHETS

Book 11

Zechariah

Part 11 of a Christian home-group
discussion course on the 12 Prophets

James Paris

Book 11:
ZECHARIAH

Historical Setting

Zechariah began his work two months after his contemporary Haggai according to Zech 1:1. This would place him about November 520 BC. Background lesson is basically the same as Haggai inasmuch as they both came down to Jerusalem with the first post exilic exiles in 536 BC. After a decree in 538 from King Cyrus who overthrew Babylon in 539. In the same way that the Lord through Jeremiah warned them of their soon coming 70 year captivity at the hands of the Babylonians. (Jer 25:7-12)
This event (the return) had been prophesised by Isaiah over 150 years earlier. (1saiah 44:24 – 45:7)

We now have the situation where Judah had been conquered 70 years earlier and taken into captivity by the Babylonians. Unlike the northern kingdom of Israel which had been taken captive by the Assyrians in 722 BC; they were settled en-mass by the Chebar river which is one reason that they were still a cohesive unit at the time of Cyrus decree. (The other being an act of God as described in Isaiah 44)

Now the Jews were to return home, however Judah was already occupied by a mixture of those who had been left behind in the exodus of 597 BC. And other groups who had in turn escaped the turmoil in their own lands to the North.

This "collective of the dispossessed" would eventually become known as the Samaritans who would become a proverbial 'thorn in the flesh' to the post exilic Israelites.

In 538 Cyrus issued a decree allowing the Jews to return to their homeland.

For more historical detail cf. the prophet Haggai.

THE BOOK

What's in a name? Zechariah means "Yahweh has Remembered"

It is a theophoric name, the ending –iah being a short Hebrew form for the Tetragrammaton. (YHWH)

Zech was himself of priestly extraction. **Zech. 1:**1 indicates he was the son of **Berechiah** and the grandson of **Iddo**. Iddo was one of the priests who returned to Jerusalem in the group led by Zerubbabel (Neh. 12:4, 16; Ezra 5:1; 6:14).

Symbolism

The book of Zechariah is possibly the most symbolic of all the Minor Prophets, with perhaps only the book of Revelations in the New Testament with as much symbolism as Zechariah. From flying Scrolls to golden lampstands, and flying Angels with wings like storks –

The Lord spoke to Zechariah in visions and symbols that defied the Prophets understanding.
Zechariah's solution to this was simply to ask the question's – and The lord answered.
In fact, in the first 6 chapters Zechariah asks no less than 10 questions regarding the visions that God was showing him. With each and every one of them, he was given an answer to clarify the vision.

Main theme - The coming Messiah.

No other prophet with the exception of Isaiah spoke more about the Messiah than Zechariah. The book is predominantly Apocalyptic and Eschatological and through his prophesies he manages to put a real awareness and eagerness into the hearts of the people with his messages of Messianic hope.
He portrays Christ in his two advents ; one as the suffering servant and the other as coming King.

Prophesies include:

- The Angel of the Lord --- 3:1
- The Righteous Branch --- 3:8; 6:12-13
- The King/Priest --- 6:13
- The humble King --- 9:9-10
- The cornerstone, tent peg, & bow of battle --- 10:4
- The Good Shepherd who is rejected & sold for 30 shekels of silver, the price of a slave --- 11:4-13
- The pierced one --- 12:10
- The cleansing fountain --- 13:1
- The smitten Shepherd who is abandoned --- 13:7
- The coming Judge & righteous King --- chapter 14

There are also Comparisons with the book of Revelations:

- The two olive trees --- Zech. 4:3f; Rev. 11:4

- **The lampstand & seven eyes --- Zech. 4:2-10; Rev. 1:12f**
- **The four horsemen --- Zech. 6:1-8; Rev. 6:1-8**

Jesus himself makes mention of Zechariah. In Matthew 23:35 and Luke 11:51 Jesus speaks of "Zechariah, the son of Berechiah" who was "murdered between the temple and the altar.".

Angels, Visions and End Times play a major role in his writings, much more so than in any other book, and apocalyptic writing is given centre stage.

Applications for Today

I believe the main thrust of Zechariah's message-the coming of the Lord-is what should drive us today, even more so than it drove the Israelites in Zechariah's time. The message of the new testament is crammed full of passages relating to the return of Christ in Power and Glory. The 'Suffering servant' has been and gone, we now await his return as the coming Judge and Righteous King (ch:14).

Eschatology – the study of the end times – is a subject that is by and large ignored today and yet the early church thought of little else. As a result the church grew at an exponential rate. This anticipation made a fertile bed for Paul and the early Apostles to sow the seed of the Gospel into.

Were they wrong to think this?
Well even during the time of the Apostles some were questioning this 'imminent' return. The Apostle Peter answered this in 2 Peter 3: 3-9 (Read).

It is not for us to know the day or hour of his return – Jesus words - (Matt 24;36. 25:13 mark 13:32) but we should be **"looking for and hastening the coming of the day of God,"**(2 Peter 3:12)
This is our Eternal Hope ! We should be more aware that we are only Pilgrims on this Earth, and eagerly anticipate the Lords return and our eternal Home.

Many Christians today have a real fear of eschatology, and shun the book of Revelations for instance, as an incomprehensible and frightening piece of literature best ignored!

Nothing could be further from the truth. The Bible is clear that one day the end of this world will come – and it won't be pretty!

We are told to make the world aware of this – and what must be done to prevent, not the end of the World, but the grisly end of the individual who does not know Jesus as their saviour.

Don't Be Afraid To Ask

Another top lesson to learn from Zechariah, is never be afraid to ask questions of The Lord. This is not the same as questioning God – far from it!

If we are confused in anyway about what The Lord desires of us, or what our next steps should be; then it is good and proper to come to The Lord and simply ask! Remember that *"The Lord has not given us a spirit of timidity, but of power and love and discipline"* **2 Tim 1:7**

Also, **Hebrews 4:16** *"Let us approach the throne with boldness.."*

Whether The Lord is speaking to you in dreams and visions, or indeed through the words within the scriptures; it is not unusual to get confused sometimes regarding the message – as in the case of Zechariah. What this book teaches us through Zechariah's example, is that it is ok to ask God for clarification, and indeed to expect The Lord to graciously make things a bit clearer for our little peanut brains to grasp!

Question 1: What do you think of Armageddon, or the end times – will it be in your lifetime?
Question 2: When was the last time you heard a message preached on the 'End Times', and would you like to hear more?
<u>And Just What Can You Do About It ?</u>

SPOTLIGHT ON THE MINOR PROPHETS
Book 12

Malachi

Part 12 of a Christian home-group discussion course on the 12 Prophets
James Paris

Book 12: MALACHI

Historical Setting.

The year is around 430 BC. The book of Malachi was written at a time of great frustration and disillusionment. Felt both by the Lord and the People of Israel.

Almost 90 years previous, the temple had been re-built by the exiles returning from the Babylonian captivity and now we have the 'third wave' of exiles led by Nehemiah. The Persian King Artaxerxes 1 gave permission for this group to return in 445 BC about 15 years previous to the writing of this book.

The situation is this – The temple has been re-built (516) the walls have been re-built (445), the priesthood has been re-established and sacrifices have re-commenced at the temple. They are reasonably secure from their enemies, all should be looking rosé!

And yet we have the reality of a corrupt priesthood (Mal 1:6-8,)who were accepting the poorest of the herd or flock for sacrifice - against the instructions of Leviticus 1v3 - and a people who had allowed themselves to submit to a 'form of religion' rather than the relationship that The Lord had called them to. Intermarriage with the heathen tribes against the express command of God (Exodus 34:12-16) was also causing problems in the exact area that The Lord warned them off.

The whole nation, Priests included had allowed themselves to become disillusioned and cynical. The natural outcome of this state of mind leads to daily worship becoming something of a chore, a job that requires to be done - as soon as you can be bothered ! this all leads to the backslidden state that we find the nation of Israel in, and sets the stage for a Prophet of the Lord to give voice to God's message…..

The Book

What's in a name? Malachi means "My Messenger" There is some debate amongst the 'learned' but it is widely accepted that Malachi was not actually the name of an individual, but rather a title. He is mentioned nowhere else by name in the Bible and Josephus who mentioned all the other 'players' in this period makes no mention of Malachi.

The writing of the book is therefore widely attributed to Ezra.

To get a fuller picture of this period it is recommended that the books of Ezra and Nehemiah be read in full.

The book of Malachi is written in quite a unique way called 'didactic' also known as 'disputation', 'assertion –objection—rebuttal '

The Lord through Malachi first makes an assertion to the people, an objection is then raised by the hearers, and finally a rebuttal or refutation is made by the speaker.

Example…Ch. 1; I have loved you," says the LORD But you say, "How have You loved us?" "Was not Esau Jacob's brother?" declares the LORD "Yet I have loved Jacob;

Through this method God chooses to break through the apathy and unbelief that has overcome the people. Always desiring a sinner to come to repentance the Lord throughout this book seeks to emphasise the danger that they are in if they stay on their present course.

God is merciful ;(Joel 2:12-14) (Rend your hearts and not your garments and return to the Lord, your God, for He is gracious and merciful, slow to anger, and abounding in loving-kindness; and He revokes His sentence of evil [when His conditions are met].

Through his ministry via Malachi he persuades at least some of the people to repentance and they even put their name in a book of remembrance (3;16)

The book ends by calling the people to revive again the teachings of Moses and by promising that Elijah will return before the 'day of the Lord'
It was another 400 years before The Lord spoke to his people again........
John the Baptist was **Elija**h according to the teachings of Jesus I Matt:11:14 "if you are willing to receive and accept it, John himself is **Elijah** who was to come" [before the kingdom].

Applications for Today

The people on their return to the 'Promised land' were set a great challenge, to re-build a ruined country.
After granted a fair amount of prodding they set about it and got on with the task of re-building the Temple and the city walls.
But look what happens when the task is completed.

- ➢ **Boredom** – We've done our job, now what?
- ➢ **Apathy** – let's just do our religious duty then get on with real life!
- ➢ **Rebelliousness** - Look at our neighbours the Canaanites, they're partying and having a great time of it !!

Proverbs 29:18 says *'Where there is no vision, the* **people perish***: but he that keepeth the law, happy is he.'* **The NIV** says –*"Where there is no revelation, the people cast off restraint; but blessed is he who keeps the law"*

The Lord knows that if we are not heading somewhere then we are going nowhere !!

We need purpose in our lives – we need the **reality** of **God** to rule in our lives and we need more than anything a <u>God Given Goal</u> a vision, a revelation, a dream that the Lord would plant in our hearts, we need to fulfil the destiny that The Lord has planned for us otherwise, like the people of Israel we will wander off into the sunset and slide into apathy and rebellion.

Last Point – people will often say of a church or individual that they have "stagnated", grown cold. I would suggest that in reality there is no such option for a christian; to 'stagnate' is to die for that is where it eventually leads.

Only by 'pressing on towards the goal' by 'keeping the faith', can we hope to get the very best out of this life that God has given us.

A quick Rant

Malachi is very often used by preachers to beat their people over the head, when it comes to tithing.

It can be fairly guarenteed for instance that any sermon that includes the subject of tithing to the Church will include this passage from Malachi 3:16 *"Bring the whole tithe into the storehouse, so that there may be food in My house, and test Me now in this," says the* LORD *of hosts, "if I will not open for you the windows of heaven and pour out for you a blessing until it overflows."*

There are a number of things to note here,

- This is an Old Testament injunction. A New Covenent Christian will not be blessed according to their obedience to an Old Covenent law!
- If we are to follow the injunctions of the Old Testament or Covenant then we are cursed

already according to the Apostle Paul in Galations 3:10 *"For as many as are of the works of the law are under the curse: for it is written, Cursed is every one that continues not in all things which are written in the book of the law to do them."*

- Malachi 3:8-10 say's that we are cursed if we do not tithe, and yet as Christians,Jesus has set us free from the curse of the Law. Gal 3:13
- If this passage is to be taken as relevant, then it would seem that God's blessing's are conditional on our tithing; which would mean in turn that His love is conditional – not unconditional as is the case according to Romans 5:8.
- If you want to get involved with Old Testament tithing, then forget the idea of 10% - it is reckoned that when everything is taken into account an Old Testament Jew would tithe around 40% of their income to the Temple!

I could go on – but this is just a quick rant ☺
There are many reasons to tithe or give to the church, I do believe it is right and there are many scriptures that point to supporting the Church in this way; however **Malachi is not one of them !**

Question: What do you think – is Tithing according to Malachi, scriptural for a New Covenant Christian?

Question: What other scriptures can be used to support giving financially to the church?

Question: What can you do if your love for the Lord has grown cold?

*****

Resources

Resources for this work are the 12 individual Minor prophets books; along with my own experiences combined with of course, internet research.

Feedback from the Bible study groups at my own home, where this course was taught, have been invaluable here and a real encouragement to go ahead with this publication.
My thanks to everyone involved.

A particular thanks for the great artwork goes to my good friend Agnieszka Gorak. You can see more examples of her unique sense of humor and observations on life at her website
http://myguineapigtales.co.uk

www.TheBibleBrief.com

Lightning Source UK Ltd.
Milton Keynes UK
UKHW02f1846190118
316494UK00005B/273/P